CATEGORICALLY SPEAKING

A Collection of Poems

ALEXANDRA MOSS ZANNIS

Order this book online at www.trafford.com
or email orders@trafford.com

Most Trafford titles are also available at major online book retailers.

Printed in the United States of America.

ISBN: 978-1-4669-4126-7 (sc)
ISBN: 978-1-4669-4125-0 (e)

Library of Congress Control Number: 2012909917

Trafford rev. 06/08/2012

 www.trafford.com

North America & international
toll-free: 1 888 232 4444 (USA & Canada)
phone: 250 383 6864 ♦ fax: 812 355 4082

CONTENTS

LIFE

The Open Wound 1

The Leaf of Life 2

Who Was She? 4

I Am Woman 5

Color Me 6

Tongue-In-Cheek 7

Anger's Whetting Stone 8

A Fetus in Cadiz 9

The Masticator 10

The Dark Cell 11

Despair 12

Old Age's Denial 13

The Old Purse 15

Cocooned 17

Mimi's Prayer 18

The Mournful Reed 19

LOVE

Trilogy on Love 20

The Remembered Kiss 21

Fusion 22

The Plague of Love 23

Forbidden Love 24

The Possession 25

Comparison 26

Song of Despair 27

Metamorphosis 28

We 29

Chips Within the Stone 30

Burning 31

Sans Regret 32

Eye of the Beholder 33

The Sweetest Song 34

The Web 35

You Speak With Forked Tongue 36

The Last of the Wild Oats 37

Closure 39

POLITICAL

Hail Kissinger! 40

With These Pledges 41

Blood Letting 42

A Tyrant's Death: Praise be to Allah? 43

Crossing the Aisle 44

Herding Sheep 45

Save This Seed! 46

Mississippi's Measure 26 47

NATURE

Ode to the Dandelion 48

Comparing Crowns...49

Farewell to Summer..50

Song of the Cicadas..51

The Nightingale's Lullaby 52

Prostate Rain...53

The Gentle Rain..54

Winter Shadows..55

Give In To The Night 56

The Tears of the Earth 57

The Dance of the Dust Ball...59

Drought 61

Schisms 62

Onslaught 63

DEATH

Mourning...64

Lamentation 65

The Immortal Tree 67

In Memory 68

The Final Flight...69

The Irrevocable 70

I Walked in Your Shadow 71

Shades of Pain...72

Tear Down the Shrine! 73

The Brilliance of the Stars 74

Bones 75

Homophobia 76

Lazarus Resurrected 77

The Last Farewell..79

Without Hope..80

HUMOR

My Father Wore Trojans 81

A Preference of Bedding 83

Nobody Came to my Funeral..84

The Last Bequest...85

Masochistic Love 86

I Drink to Death 87

The Itch to Plant? 88

The Pleasures of Scotch 89

Curiosity..90

The Joys of Winter 91

In a 'Clintonized' Manner...92

No Tears for Monica 93

The Joy of a Youthful Bladder 94

My Old House..95

SATIRICAL SONNETS

To a Cleavage 96

A Joyful Ending..97

True Love 98

Love's Competition..99

The Shrinking Skirt..100

The Designer Man 101

The Age of Cloning 102

The Marriage Vows..103

The Holy Word..104

The Playboy Centerfold 105

The Serpent 106

Fossils..107

THE OPEN WOUND

We are forced into life
through the open wound,
smeared with its blood
and entangled in its placental snare.

Each day of our lives
we are impaled and gored
by the relentless traumas
that pierce our inescapable net.

The wound is within us,
never healing, but seeping
with the blood and tears
of our infinite sorrows.

THE LEAF OF LIFE

How deliciously iridescent was the budding leaf
when it burst into bloom on an extruding limb of the tree—
another leaf sprouting forth from those that preceded it;
another leaf to burden the boughs of that time-worn tree;
an added weight until it no longer could bear life's fruit.

But what a tiny leaf—no danger to fell the tree, no danger
to bend the bough to the bone-filled earth. I shimmered
and glowed from the dew that caressed me at sunrise,
bouncing and dancing from the touch of the morning breeze,
singing as the surging sap filled my tiny veins;

I expanded and thrived in the sun's dappling shadows,
growing rich and lustrous with the cleansing of the rain,
expanding into an age-ripened leaf able to comprehend
my identity among the fledgling leaves, able to sense
my uniqueness among the flowering branches.

Then one day, bursting with the strength of my youth,
I tore away from my roots, snapped the stem that held me
and leaped onto the winds of flight that bore me upwards
and onwards into the swirling currents of life.
Freed from my umbilical cord, I soared into the future.

Aspiring heaven and seeking to reach unimagined heights,
I strained to devour all the delights presented by the wind.
I soared into maturity with each season stealing a piece
of my life-giving fluids until, as a waning leaf,
I began to shrivel and wilt from my pleasure-seeking years.

When the buoyant winds no longer could lift my dying cells,
I began to swirl and twirl downward into the twilight
of brittle decay, falling to the ground beneath
the time-worn tree where once I budded and bloomed
with life. Curling into myself I became one with the earth.

WHO WAS SHE?

Who was that little girl who shed that diminutive body
like a cocoon emerging into the inception of its life?
Is she but a diaphanous memory her mind grasps upon
when the gravity of life casts doubt upon her being?

Who was she, all those years ago, who flung
those tiny arms around her mother's waist
remembering the softness of that stomach
which had been her embryonic cradle?

Who was that little girl whose father's songs
implanted in that untilled mind a hereditary seed
that bloomed into a voice of unimagined dreams?

Who was that little child, that tiny sapling
that sprouted into another form of being; a dandelion
that vegetated on the earth whose flower head
detached and floated on the winds of life?

Who was that little girl who now is but a dream;
that ova-sperm that germinated into what she is today
and now not knowing who once she used to be?

I AM WOMAN

I am as strong as the morning sun
that bursts upon the earth each day.
It never changes, never tires, never ages.

I am older than the Bristlecone pines that stand
invincible in the noonday sun's scorching,
the wind's raging, the rain's drenching.

I am the fertile ground for ripening fruit;
I am the bearer of man's continuing seed,
the flowering soil, absorber of the rain.

I am as ageless as time, unyielding to death,
eternal youth that thrives upon the earth.
I am me! I am life! I am WOMAN!

COLOR ME

If you hate me, color me black
like the bottomless cavity of hell
and let no sunlight seep into the abyss;
or inject my soul with India ink
and wrathfully write the word "bitch"
upon its assailable substance.

If you resent me, color me green
like the burning envy in your eyes
as you stare covetously at me,
or green like the bubbling bile
that ceaselessly churns and grinds
in the pit of your embittered bowels.

If you love me, make me brilliant
like the rays of the sun igniting
the dancing ripples on a lucid lake
into glistening gems, or color me
fuchsia like the wild rose that blooms
in spring without ostentation.

If you leave me colorless
then I am faceless, bodiless
and soulless—invisible to the world.
So take your pallet of paints and color me
the pigments of hate, envy or love,
for then I am visible in your eyes.

TONGUE-IN-CHEEK

Here you sit within my mouth,
you pretender of wit, arched
to spring forth with some
diabolically cynical witticism.

Even when you're forced into the hollow
of my cheek I feel you throbbing
as you preen yourself
to ejaculate into articulation.

And then, like a flying javelin,
you hurl yourself from the safety
of my cheek and pierce
the conversation with your poison.

O, tongue, shall I call upon Tereus
to surgically dispose of you
as he did Philamela?
    . . . . but I fear the bird would become a vulture!

ANGER'S WHETTING STONE

No human face, but molten flesh
that melted into devilish form
with each vile utterance!

Bulbous eyes that seared into my own
and from their depths unleashed the furies
of a thousand dormant hates.

Surly lips, curled back in wolf-like snarl,
could not restrain the spittle from his mouth
that dribbled like hot coals down his chin;

Hands stiffened into clenched fists,
upraised and hungry for the satiable feel
of dented flesh and smashing bone.

I felt the anger well up within my throat
like bile; a bitter vetch that chocked my voice
and made me puke my words out in that face.

And then it came! The smashing fist!
My gasp for breath exploding with surprise
from shock and fear and hate.

A FETUS IN CADIZ

When first she knew her womb was generating life
her body seemed to levitate above the ground.
She felt herself afloat within a magic spume,

not knowing then the seed within was not to be.
The sperm provider vowed for total termination;
and the devastating serum found its tiny target.

While in Cadiz the extrication first began.
She moaned aloud in lacerating agony,
cold sweat pouring down her pain-contorted face.

The inert fetus, liberated from its tomb,
lay lifeless in her palm—so small a thing,
no larger than the graphic image of a tadpole.

For burial, it was flushed into the toilet,
swirling down into the sewers of Cadiz;
a victim of rejection, lost in the pits of hell.

THE MASTICATOR

(with apologies to Omar Khayyam)

I sat across from her fascinated,
no, hypnotized, as I watched her mouth
gnashing up and down on her food,
moving two scrunches per second.

She had thin lips, maybe an inch
beneath her long nose that looked
like an arrow pointing to a mouth
that never stopped masticating..

When she halted long enough to talk,
her mouth opened like a sewer grate,
the salivary juices running down
the sides trying to escape her teeth.

If we could see ourselves as others see us,
would there exist idealistic poetry?
Would Omar Khayyam in his Rubaiyat
have changed "T*he moving finger having writ . . .*"
to:

The masticating mouth does chew
and having chewed gnaws on, nor all
its gnashing nor its grinding shall eradicate
one morsel from it's culinary function?

THE DARK CELL

I have condemned all those dreams
that dissipated into disappointments
and never-to-be achieved into that dark
and airless cell deep within my heart.
I have thrust them in, squeezing them
like festering pus in a pustule wound,
without hope of ever being released.

Those dreams that contorted the lifeline
to my heart, that forced my tears to flow
like lava from a ruptured volcano,
that compelled my voice to shriek
in soundless screams, I shove
into that cell and dance upon their grave!

DESPAIR

The sun will rise no more
upon the mornings of her world.
No longer will it permeate
the droplets of the morning dew;
no longer will it dry
the mildew of despair
that coats her troubled mind.

The moon will rise no more
upon the darkness of her world.
No longer will it infuse
the night that shrouds her mind
like the mourning mantles
of the wailing widows who
plod unseeing in the streets.

OLD AGE'S DENIAL

They sat at the breakfast table, an old
tired couple with their guest, reminiscing
on their youth. She had forgotten the passions
that once had boiled inside her blood;
he remembered, but his blood no longer
surged through his narrow veins.

"Sex is the greatest force in the world,"
spoke up their youthful companion.
"Oh, no!" cried the old woman, "how
can you say that! It's only for procreation!"
She spent her old age reading the worn
pages of her Bible, preparing for death.

"Wife", retorted her husband, "have you
forgotten your youth and our nights of love?
Why do you deny those memories
that ripened our union?" He was older
and more disabled than she, but his mind
had not forgotten his memories of youth.

"Husband," she replied, "the Devil is gnawing
at your heart. The mind must not
give in to the sin of bodily pleasures."
What pity! She could no longer recall
their nights of heated, passionate love
that soaked their ardent bodies with sweat.

"Poor wife, you deny the pleasures of our youth?
In front of our guest you proclaim yourself
a frigid woman? God will not condemn you
for reliving those moments of love. If sex
had no sweetness or pleasure, there would be
no conjoining and no procreation."

The old woman lowered her head, casting
her eyes unseeing upon the table.
She had no response to give her husband;
no holy utterance came to mind to refute
his words of truth. She remembered
those nights, but in recalling them now
felt guilty of betraying the virtue of old age.

THE OLD PURSE

She walks slowly down the street, her purse
clutched close to her thin, flaccid breast.
It's a purse whose color is hard to determine.
Its leather is worn thin and its straps seem
to cling exhaustedly to the clasp. She's afraid
to loosen her grasp, afraid if it were snatched
from her, her world would be destroyed.

Passing the flower vendor on the street,
she looks longingly at the clusters of lilacs
that fill the air with their earthy fragrant smell.
They remind her of her youth when they bloomed
free for the picking. She no longer
can afford to pay for them. She keeps
their memory sealed in her mind and walks on.

Entering the small neighborhood market, she shuffles
slowly through the aisles, noting the prices, determining
what she can afford to buy. No money for the red,
glistening beef lying temptingly in the glass case,
no money for fresh fruits or vegetables. She passes
all these and resolutely goes to the "reduced price" section.
She must settle for what little money she has.

Opening her pocketbook, she counts the few bills and coins,
disappointment lining her face. So little for luxuries,
so little even for necessities. She chooses dented cans
of vegetables, chipped beef, some fruits, a small package
of tea whose cellophane wrapping has been ripped.
Eyes straight ahead, she pushes the cart towards
the check-out counter, laying upon it her poor purchases.

With gnarled fingers, she opens her worn purse and carefully
counts the money she must give up for such insufficient essentials.
Picking up the parcel, she clutches her purse close to her breast,
walking hurriedly out the grocery, passing the lilacs unseeing.
Arriving home, she lays her pocketbook on the bureau. Rubbing
her hand over the worn leather, as if caressing a loved one,
she whispers "May I never find you empty, old friend.".

COCOONED

I wove it around me, snug and secure,
invisible to the world pressing upon me,
not wanting curious eyes to penetrate
this protective panoply I was spinning.

I spun it slowly, year by year, each knot
in the tracery reinforced to shield me
from the doubts and insecurities
that shrieked to impale my dubious ego.

I wanted no weaknesses to be discovered,
no Achilles heel where words, like poisoned
darts, could penetrate the armor I so tenaciously
had twined around my fragilities.

I wound it so tightly no one could peer in
to spy upon the secrets I had hidden there.
I wound it and forgot I needed a window
from which I could escape my own deceptions.

MIMI'S PRAYER

(Based on the Opera La Bohême by Puccini)

I fear I'll die before the healing sun of Spring
Arrives to thaw the mucus in my frozen chest.
There is no heat within my tiny squalid room
To counteract the wind that seeps in so grotesque
A manner, turning into hoarfrost everything.

My frigid fingers pain when trying to create
The artificial flowers I construct to sell
Upon the corners of the narrow snow-slushed streets.
The consumptive cough that wracks my lungs I cannot quell;
There is no other course for me to contemplate.

Rodolfo, once the sun that warmed my frozen heart,
No longer tolerates the bondage of my love.
I'm now unbearably alone in my despair,
No one to care or understand the why thereof
I live or die, no one to weep when I depart.

Oh, Spring, let me survive to see once more the sun
Rise up above the Paris roofs; to feel its heat
Inflate my lungs with healing breaths and let me live
To know once more Rodolfo's love. So bitter-sweet
Is life. Dear God, just let me feel once more the sun!

Alexandra Moss Zannis

THE MOURNFUL REED

He sits cross-legged on the shadowed grass,
eyes turned inward to that sacred place
where he alone can probe the mystery
of the spirit world. He gently strokes
the perforations in the ancient flute,
each readjustment of his touch evokes

an image of his ancestral tribe
who sat around an eerie, smoking fire,
their faces dancing in and out of shadows
in that ghostly, flickering flame. Now he alone
plays softly on his mournful reed,
evoking visions from his tribal past.

TRILOGY ON LOVE

Come, lie beside me on my bed,
No one will see our fervid kiss.
I draw the shade on prying eyes
By forsaking all for this.

*   *   *

Love's greatest sinner am I when
I lay myself upon your bed.
But what would be the greater sin,
To love, or silence love instead?

*   *   *

Sweet hell, that calms my burning breast
And brings release unto my mind,
What heaven could I ever seek
If I must leave this hell behind!

THE REMEMBERED KISS

O, how I loved you, my love, Your kiss
unsealed my heart and it came pouring out
to you like ripples in a lake circling closer
and closer about you until it bound me
to you, never to be freed.

Without you there is no life, my love,
without you the days are nights
and the nights are endless tunnels
of memories with every heartbeat
reverberating like the crashing of waves
upon the barren beaches of loneliness.

Always love me, my love, for you are as the rain
quenching my arid soul, and if the rain
should stop, the flower blooms no more.

FUSION

Come, lie beside me; whisper fantasies
that only lovers dare to speak about.
Let us weave our bodies into a plait
of searing, supple flesh, so tightly wound
that it can only be unraveled by the calming,
soothing balm of love's depletion.

Come, soar with me to unimagined heights
where soul and body levitate above
their planetary shackles, hovering
within the realm of ecstasies known only
by those endowed with esoteric dreams—
that overpowering fusion of fervid flesh

THE PLAGUE OF LOVE

(Terza Rima)

Ah, love! She's sick with the disease. She roams
Throughout her days unseeing of the moon,
The sun, her mind obsessed with love's sweet tomes.

The stars could blaze within an afternoon
And neutralize the brilliance of the sun
But to this awe, her eyes would be immune.

The wind could scream across the earth and none
Could tolerate its devastating roar,
Yet she would only hear the songs he'd sung.

Black clouds could mass like armies off to war
Transforming heaven's sunlight into night,
Though she alone would glow with love's décor

The rain could drench the earth with all its might
Creating raging rivers, surging seas,
But she would merely float in loves delight.

Ah, love! She's sick with this unwanted plague
But has no wish to end this vain charade.

FORBIDDEN LOVE

I blame no Eden. I blame no snake
when that lustful apple was offered to me
in those two appealing outstretched hands.
It lay seductively savory and ripe
with the promise of hidden, succulent juices.

I looked beyond those masculine hands
into the eyes of the proffer, and drowned
in the depths of his hypnotic gaze.
I grasped the fruit with trembling fingers
and devoured it like a ravenous beast.

I blame no Eden, I blame no snake—
I knew the fruit for the poison it bore.

THE POSSESSION

Give me this head that towers
so stately on its manly throne;
these lips, which molded pouting,
spread like angel wings
in laughter's exaltation;

this nose, so noble in protrusion,
expounding to the world
its Grecian claim; these eyes,
which bear the sadness
of the world, yet cannot find relief

in sorrow's tears. Give me this face,
untouched by anger's grinding stone,
to gaze upon, enraptured, as I see it now
composed within the purity of love.

COMPARISON

Other hands have touched me,
Hands for me alone.
Other arms have held me,
Arms as strong as stone.

Other eyes I've looked in,
Eyes that shone for me,
But never have I seen such eyes
That gazed so tenderly.

Other men have kissed me
With lips that were more true.
Other men have loved me
But not half so sweet as you.

SONG OF DESPAIR

Don't look in my eyes
And don't try to surmise
What emotions I hide.
My heart is a tomb
In a windowless room
Where love has died.

I'm so tired of losin',
This so-called illusion's
Not even a game.
I've no more a heart left
Not even a spark left
To fan a flame.

Love pass me by.
My heart wants no share
Of that aching despair
On the day when two lovers depart.

Oh, love, pass me by.
Let me breathe the free air
Of a platonic affair;
Let my mind have the rule of my heart.

METAMORPHOSIS

Old flesh clasping the flesh of youth; veined hands
caressing the solidity of a body still congealed
in the ripeness of youth; fingers seeking to find
what once she was but wasting now into human decay.

The ultimate joy of her diminishing world is to touch
this sinewy masculine body, to stroke each mound
of durable flesh extruding from his stalwart manly form,
to feel the strength of his youthful body rejuvenating hers.

She feels the ardor of passion flowing through her aging body
like a typhoon cleansing a littered shore. Her youth
is here once more, grasped within her flaccid arms;
pressed like searing metal against her hollow breasts.

WE

How lovely rings the sound of 'we'
Now that we've joined the 'you' and 'me'
To form this sweet simplicity.

No longer am I just an 'I,'
Or speak of ownership as 'my';
It's now to 'ours' that I reply.

CHIPS WITHIN THE STONE

I thought each man I loved was carved from stone,
or if not stone, then solid as an oak
that spreads its sturdy limbs like shielding arms
above my head to ward off any harm
befalling me. Foolish were my dreams.

Little did I understand those men
had weaknesses as I, but that I did
not want to see. I sought a God within
each one and when I peered beneath the mask
I saw the chips that marred the God I sought.

Those godly men, whose visions I decreed
as my salvation, shriveled in my sight,
revealing them as merely mortal men—
no God for me to idolize
with their crumbling feet of earth-bound clay.

BURNING

He appears in my sleep, forcing me to relive
this passion I've never been able to forget,
this flame he won't let die, but keeps
rekindling with his night-time stalking
in my slumber-drugged delusions.

When he retreats from my dreams, I forget
the madness I wallowed in. I forget my despair
when I could not be with him, when my desire
went unshared and I suffered loneliness.
Sweet slumber when my soul is my own.

But he follows me, never letting me escape
the emotion he once set ablaze in my heart.
He returns from his heaven or hell
to imprison me with his memory,
refusing to give up this earthly possession.

He tracks me in silence, neither speaking
nor touching, and yet I feel his branding iron
always pressing against my heart,
cauterizing me as his property, unwilling
to release this passion he infused in me.

He possesses me. The flame he once kindled,
the flame I had forced myself to quench,
resurges, burning in me like a fiery torch,
forcing me to relive all the lust and sorrow
I once groveled-in. I burn, I burn.

SANS REGRET

My mother said *"You've made your bed now lie in it!"*
So now I lie alone in the bed I made in haste
when I devised my destiny: the eternal bed,
always changing form, giving no solaced sleep.

My mother made her bed, a bed that brought
her tears and disillusionment. She bore that bed
like Atlas shouldering the world. She never cried
"mistake!", she knew it was the bed she chose.

So many different beds I've made: some, as like
St. Paul, where painful thorns thrust into my flesh;
some like rocks weighing heavily on my conscience;
then others that lured me into spurious dreams.

To these, my beds, so stained with atrabilious tears,
that bore the fervent sweat of overzealous love;
that brought no comfort to my agitated heart,
I say: *"Sweet beds, sans regret, sans regret".*

EYE OF THE BEHOLDER

Your beauty fills my eyes to overflowing;
I know not why, you are no fair Adonis
who with his hypertrophic beauty
drove Persephone and Aphrodite
to wage a war for absolute possession;

nor is your beauty one romantic poets
immortalize. Yours is that baffling beauty
surrounding you with an iridescent aura,
a glow reflecting what your soul portrays:
a radiant inextinguishable flame

You are the perfect form filling my sight,
eradicating all inconsequential visions
flitting past my blinded eyes,
and in the chambers of my heart
you are the love banishing all others.

THE SWEETEST SONG

I sing no more, Oh, weary world,
So burdened by the voice of man,
I close my lips on tonal sounds
And let no music flow again.

I lock all lyrics in my heart
From where they whisper love to me;
For what songs could I sing aloud
That would in silence sweeter be?

THE WEB

He wove it well, his silken web,
so fine the human eye could barely see
the tiny threads crisscrossing one upon the other.
It shone with blinding effulgence and changed
its sleek contour with hypnotic vacillation.

She realized her folly much too late
and when she understood, she had no will
to free herself from that entanglement.
She dangled like the hanged man
of the Tarot cards, but not with his perception

of the circumstances surrounding her.
She was entwined among those silken threads,
too blinded by the ardor in her eyes,
too weak to comprehend his artful vise—
a victim of her sensuous desires.

YOU SPEAK WITH
FORKED TONGUE

You speak to me with forked tongue, my Love,
intriguing my ears with your words of love flying off
in two directions. I'm fascinated by your tongue
flicking left and right like a lizard's, your left prong

slurping up those sweet words like delectable insects
uttered by your right. They soar like Eros' poisoned
tipped arrows, spoken in coy deceit; ingested
before they can ring with insincerity into my ears.

Someday, my Love, I'll attack like a snake
that flicking tongue of yours and bite it out
of your mouth so no one else can be stung
by the devious duplicity of your forked tongue.

Alexandra Moss Zannis

THE LAST OF THE WILD OATS

The jar was full so many years ago,
But thinking it more wise to be discrete
I only flung a handful sparingly—
Upon a pair of eyes that shone with love,

A smiling mouth that curved like angel's wings
As laughter rang like music from his throat.
When once I flung the oats too carelessly
The wind returned the grains with such a force

My eyes were blinded by the gust until
My tears exposed the folly of my deed.
Then wisely did I watch the coursing winds
Before I sowed my wild misguided seeds

The jar now had so little left to hoard
I thought it best to close the battered lid,
But when I thought *Why harbor such a few?*
I turned and threw the last into the wind.

With some regret but knowing that at last
I'd freed myself from love's uncertainty,
I cleansed my mind of all entanglements
And chose to walk the path of chastity.

Then suddenly those seedlings I had scorned
And tossed away with grim decisiveness
Returned with such a force my body reeled,
For love appeared and filled my hollow heart.

Don't think of love as only for the young:
It comes to anyone who has no fear
Of throwing to the wind those last few seeds
That in that jar lay dormant through the years.

Alexandra Moss Zannis

CLOSURE

All has been written,
the pen moves no more.
Were the words
fingered in the sand
and washed out to sea
with the outgoing tide?

There is no trace of their existence.
No letters, no pressed flowers
hidden in envelopes,
no photographs
as a remembrance
of what had been.

Only the distant echo
of a song playing
its sentiment over and over,
a tortuous melody
as a reminder of passion
that once existed:

a tapestry of love
woven in illusionary knots
now unraveling
into the deceptive dust of death.
The last page is read.
The book is closed.

HAIL KISSINGER!

(Written in memory of the Cyprus invasion)

Hail, Kissinger, defender of the Turks! You flaunt
their wreath of poppies on your head as if it were
a crown of royal jewels. But in your hands the flag
of peace implants their seeds of death among our youth.

New, self-hypnotized Paraclete, it's not
the hand of God that motivates your roguish course,
but megalomaniac powers burning deep to hue
your egotistic smoke-hallucinated dreams.

Beware, O bungling barrister, of your mistake
in spurning noble Greece—once brother, ally, succor
to our cause. It will not always play the pawn
in your ostentatious game of world chess!

WITH THESE PLEDGES . . . .

(Dissention to the Iraqi Invasion)

I pledge allegiance to the aggression
for which we stand. One nation impulsively
forcing our freedom on other nations
that wish we'd keep our belligerence at home!

I pledge allegiance to the CIA
and the FBI to patrol the world
in search of non-conforming leaders
who refuse to play by the rules we've ordained

I pledge to rout out all dissidents to our cause,
even with covert war. I pledge to bomb
their presumptuous dissensions
and to destroy their dreams of autonomy.

I pledge to uphold the stars and stripes
which "In God We Trust" controls the world.
We are the only God-appointed nation
to force our beliefs upon the heathens.

I pledge allegiance to the blood we must shed
to uphold our supremacy over the "infidels,"
even to the economic destruction of the freedom
founded by our peacemaking forefathers!

BLOOD LETTING

Watch it pour from the wounds of our youth
as they lie dying on the battlefield for democracy;
a democracy that cannot be understood or accepted
by the enemy—an enemy that was created by us,
and for what intent? There were no weapons
of mass destruction, there was no terrorism
when we invaded that land.

Was it in retaliation for the failure of his father
to rid Iraq of a sadistic dictator, or was it
for the purpose of controlling the precious
black gold that flowed from its fields
to replenish our shrinking supply?

Like a fresh-dug oil well, our youth's blood
spurted skyward and fell back to earth
defeating the name of democracy
because of the whim of an egotistical
president who dreamed of immortality.

Will his immortality be carved upon the stone
slab of history as the 43rd President
of the United States of America who opened
the fissures of the dam that protected democracy
and drowned our country in hate and retribution?

A TYRANT'S DEATH:
PRAISE BE TO ALLAH?

Accused of killing thousands Iraqis
he stood on the witness stand defying
the judicial system. What audacity—
an accused man, claiming still
his presidency of a defeated land!

    . . . . Praise be to Allah.

Hanged for his crimes, clasping
the Koran and reciting an Islamic prayer,
the knotted rope was wrapped
around his neck. He stood hoodless
and defiant in the face of death.

    . . . . "Ya Allah", he claimed.

Amid the scream of "Go to hell!"
the floor opened, plunging him to his death . . .

    . . . . Praise be to Allah?

CROSSING THE AISLE

It's not that wide, but not like crossing
the Verrazano-Narrows Bridge spanning
the Hudson River. Still, it's a big step,
one that takes a lung full of oxygen
and a willingness to extend your hand.

Is it more productive to blow spit balls
at each other across the aisle, hoping your aim
is as accurate as using telescopic lens
for a direct hit that will paralyze your opponent
into submitting to *your* preferred platform?

If the red and the blue merged, it would become
the noble and spiritual color of purple.
What more would we want from our legislators
but to walk shoulder to shoulder and work
hand in hand to accomplish miracles..

So, get off your Brooks Brothers clad butts,
place those Cesare Paciotti shoes on the floor,
point them to that aisle of dissention,
take that stalwart step towards collaboration
and perform the job the people demand.

HERDING SHEEP

Come! Follow me. Gather around.
I will lead you to pastures of clover emersed;
Where cooling springs bubble up through the ground
Quenching your querying, insatiable thirst.

I will take you to meadows not grazed before,
To lands overflowing with opulent grain,
To places no creatures have dared to explore,
Where ceaseless prosperity fills the domain.

No longer you'll reach for those dubious dreams,
They're eagerly waiting the clasp of your hand.
It's all you imagined and more than it seems:
This vision I promise to every man.

Believe what I tell you it comes from my heart,
These pastures of clover to which I allude.
You'll never lament this course that I chart
But forever will hail me with deep gratitude.

Come! Follow me. Open your eyes,
Look closely at me, I wear no disguise
For I'm as American as apple pie;
The true Politician who'll never lie!

SAVE THIS SEED!

Save this seed! Let this child be born
into the pit of perpetual poverty;
let it cope with pestilence and hunger;
let it suffer inhumanity,
but give it birth to know the joy of strife!

Why do men who have no womb to bear
a seed and women who know no poverty
enforce their rules upon the destitute
who cannot voice their rights and must in silence
bear the seed that grows within their wombs?

You say to kill an embryo is against
the will of God. You preach that life is sacred,
but to whom? Do you ask the woman
wearied by the drudgery of endless
childbearing? An unwed pregnant girl?

No, you are without compassion! You shout:
"Let this embryo live to endure abuse,
but don't abort this seed! Let this embryo
live to endure injustice and starvation,
but do **not** abort this sacred seed!"—
. . .*for God so loved the world?*

Alexandra Moss Zannis

MISSISSIPPI'S MEASURE 26

I heard him say, this man
from Mississippi, to use
any form of contraception
is murder. Even if the woman
is put in danger, let her die!
His seed is more important.

Oh, the vanity of this man
who thinks his sperm
so supreme it takes preference
over a woman's existence.
She is nothing more than a vessel
to fulfill his egotistical control.

I say to him "spill it on the ground"
and let it fertilize the soil
that soon will become so barren
it can no longer feed the mouths
of the billions more unwanted souls
whom your seeds will create.

ODE TO THE DANDELION

Oh, selfish yellow springtime child
that augments so prolifically,
You spread your seeds in arrogance
And dare the earth to disagree.

You raise your tendriled yellow head
And wantonly vociferate:
I'll conquer all without regard,
The land is mine to propagate

You paint the fields so lavishly
They shimmer with your color gold.
You nod and smile within the wind
And think you noble to behold.

But there are those who have no care
For all the swagger you assume,
You're much more tender to digest
Before you burgeon into bloom

So vain, conceited dandelion
Beware the culinarians.
They'll roughly pull you from the ground
To feed the vegetarians.

COMPARING CROWNS

Like the head of a bald old man,
the tree begins to lose its foliage
at the top of its crown. Each leaf,
one by one as a strand of hair,
pulls away from its dying roots,
laying bare the upper branches,
resembling a hairless skull.

The bottom leaves remain,
likening to the circular fringe
of hair clinging to the naked pate,
until a heavy frost freezes the pores
and then they, too, lose their grip
and flutter down onto the cold ground,
leaving the tree stripped of adornment.

Laid bare to arctic winds, the tree
shivers without its protective foliage.
The bald man wears a warm covering
around his head. But the barren tree
needs only wait 'til Spring to re-grow
its crowning glory. The hairless pate
of the old man will never know rebirth.

FAREWELL TO SUMMER

How sweet it was when Summer tempered
the winds of Spring, perfuming the air
with its hedonic scents of the greening earth.
The leaves burgeoned like the beauty
of a pregnant woman anticipating with joy
the life growing within her swelling womb.

The ponds and lakes, warmed by the embrace
of the doting sun, lured the transient birds
onto their healing waters to gather strength
for their long flight in following the sun
as it forsook the northern shores, returning
to its pivotal point of equatorial origin.

Then the funereal fifes of Fall rang loud
their dirge as slowly the lid of Summer's coffin
closed and, like a stealthy thief, the cold winds
of Winter waited to spring upon Fall's retreating back.
Farewell, sweet Summer, farewell to the healing balms
Winter will suck from the marrow of our cold bones.

SONG OF THE CICADAS

It's August and the heat of summer
presses down upon the dense
leafy trees that shade the earth:
a haven for the swarming cicadas.

The air is filled with the shrill staccato
of the males as they chant their song,
hoping to entice the females to join
with them in their last ritual of love.

It's no wonder the poor cicadas sing
so loudly and persistently. They emerge
from the earth to propagate,
lay their eggs, and then die.

So listen to their plaintive song
when the heat of summer stifles the earth.
It is not an Ode to Joy,
but a dirge for their impending death.

THE NIGHTINGALE'S LULLABY

Twilight drapes the sky with its somber colors of night
eclipsing the fading flames of the sun, preparing
heaven's stage for sunset's dramatic finale.

The sun majestically bows to its audience the sea,
and in response to the breakers' thunderous applause,
bends its head and swiftly, as an acrobatic diver,

slips into the sea creating not a ripple to disturb
the horizon's placid division of light and darkness.
The shades of night slowly draw their final curtain.

The wistful song of a solitary nightingale drifts
upon the currents of the evening breeze: a soft lullaby
lulling to sleep the setting sun in its watery cradle.

PROSTATE RAIN

It's like the bladder of an old man.
The heavens rumble, lightning flashes,
black clouds scurry across the sky,
but nothing happens. A few raindrops
fall upon the earth. That's it!

He feels the need for relief, strains
to dispense of the pressure pressing
upon him, but only a few drops
issue forth. The crisis has passed.
Nothing more can be evacuated.

Poor old man. Poor old rain!
You are one and the same. Your bladders
cannot sustain the pressure put upon you.
Whatever it held within cannot come out
and so the dribbling ends on a dry note.

THE GENTLE RAIN

It falls softly, like the tender touch of fingers
caressing the parachute ball of a dandelion,
afraid if too much pressure is applied,
the sphere will break away and float
upon the winds into obscurity.

Each drop tests its weight upon the soil,
carefully measuring the intensity of its impact
upon the arid loam, as if mindful
of the consequence of overpowering
the earth with its torrential force.

It falls gently, hour after hour,
reviving the dying grass into consciousness,
giving the outreaching roots of the trees
a reprieve from their futile search,
filling the air with its metallic smell of life.

The rain falls tenderly, as if caressing
the furrowed face of an old woman,
giving her memories of her youth
when the soil of her body
was fertile and ripe for procreation.

WINTER SHADOWS

They creep furtively across the snow, like
stealthy fingers seeking to clutch and destroy
the unblemished purity of winter's virtue.
They slither far across the meadow, forcing
their cerulean stain on the whitened ground.

Upon reaching the slumbering pond, they sink
into its unobstructed depths, invisible to the world
until the beckoning morning sun stirs them awake
to begin again their ponderous journey
over the frozen snow-covered earth.

GIVE IN TO THE NIGHT

We cannot fight the night,
nor eliminate the darkness
it spreads upon the earth.

In summer the night awaits
the sun's descent before it lazily
blocks the lingering glint of twilight.

It plunges down upon the earth
in winter like a guillotine beheading
the warmth of the sun's rays.

The weary will sigh with relief
and wedge their bodies between
its comforting covers of somnolence.

The inflicted will flounder in fear,
reliving those demons of darkness
that consume their waking hours.

Whatever plague our bodies bear,
whatever hope lies silently therein,
we cannot escape the night.

It comes tenderly or cruelly upon us.
Only the dead cannot envision it
as they lie peacefully in its depths.

Alexandra Moss Zannis

THE TEARS OF THE EARTH

How beautiful you must have been
before man slithered upon your shores:
Untouched beauty, glowing with ripeness
like the flesh of a young maiden,
iridescent as the glow of a pearl
still left in the shelter of the mollusk.

Your body unmolested, the fruits
of your womb planted by the seed
of God springing forth, growing, budding,
and flowering in the purity of innocence,
warming your green valleys and mountains
with the shimmering light of the sun.

Then man came to trod upon your soil.
First on all fours, then upright, then howling
with his supremacy over all creatures.
He dug into your mountains, drilled
into your bowels, weighed you down
with towering slabs of ugly concrete.

He slaughtered living creatures for sport,
some species never to roam the planet again,
and boasted of his superior intellect.
He warred with other nations, torturing
and killing his assumptive enemies
for maniacal control of the world.

Realizing your destruction, you fought back,
pushing the feces in your bowels upward
through the mouths of the mountains,
flexing the depths of the oceans into
churning tsunamis, prodding the winds
into horrific hurricane force.

But man would not relent his greed.
There was no repentance, no hope
for salvation. Only annihilation.
Your remorse filled the heavens with the salt
of your tears and they welled to overflow,
drowning all with your anguish.

THE DANCE OF THE DUST BALL

Pinned to the splintery post
supporting the screen on the porch,
it hung like a transparent ornament,
dejected, apathetic, yet straining
to be released from its imprisonment.

It was an accumulation of many things—
cat hairs, fibers, fluff, dirt, grime—
that had formed into a circular mass
of weightlessness, only to be entangled
in the splinters of the rough porch post.

This dust ball had no soul, no spirit.
It was an object formed to float freely
with no gravitational pull to force it
into submission. Yet, here it was
entangled in the splintery post.

Suddenly, a gust of wind pushed
through the screens, swirling within the porch,
fluttering the leaves of the potted fern,
whipping the grill's cover, and then,
finding the shackled dust ball, set it free.

It soared! It danced! The wind filled
it with buoyancy, giving it life,
letting it dance wildly across the floor.
Oh, how it rolled and twisted, vibrating
with the joy of being liberated from its shackles.

For a moment it lived. For a moment
it soared with the joy of freedom,
knowing no bounds. Then the wind died.
It fell to the floor exhausted and listless,
only to be impaled again to the post.

DROUGHT

The soil has dried into dusty particles
that sift and blow with the wind:
there is no water to compress or solidify it.
The grass has no moisture to suck upon
to fortify it with life. It is overpowered
by the tenacity of the creeping weeds
that exist without condensation.
The wails of the dying grass are stifled.

The tall stately trees are shooting out
their roots searching desperately
for life-preserving fluids. There is none.
The leaves are withering from malnutrition,
turning brown and clinging despairingly
to their branches, knowing death is near.
The strangling shrieks of the parched trees
are drowned by the clamor of humanity.

Man is oblivious to the pain of nature.
He is insensible to the silent screams
of the grass that softens his footsteps,
he is unconscious of the moaning
of the desiccated trees that caress him with shade.
Nearby are heard the pleasure-filled screams
of children wallowing in their water-filled pools
that drain the aquifer of precious water.

SCHISMS

Faults in the bowels of the earth grind
and crunch together like gnashing teeth
in a massive mouth devouring
everything in their destructive path.

The pressure of its indigestion
erodes its inflated gullet.
It spews its intolerable puke upwards,
shattering the opiate tranquility.

The land trembles and splits from the force
of its vomit. Buildings crumble like match sticks
and humanity is sucked into the chaos
and buried under tons of concrete.

After a millennium of seconds,
the deafening silence explodes with the screams
of the frenzied and despairing victims
entombed under the inescapable rubble.

ONSLAUGHT

Beware of the changing of the wind
when the clouds begin to twist
and swirl into dark concentrated masses
of spiraling scuds speeding across the sky
like frothy-mouthed stallions blind
to all else but to reach the finish line.

Watch diligently for the first sign
of a churning mass of cumulus, rotating
faster and faster, forming that huge circle,
developing into the cyclonic ferocity
that rips and tears across the land,
destroying all that stands in its path.

Sharpen your hearing to catch the first
warning of this catastrophic storm:
the shrill shriek of the sirens, their sound
fading in and out as they turn directionally,
or the frantic tolling of the church bells
clanging with alarm the impending doom.

Run, run before the vortex of the storm
sucks you up into its barbarous bowels.
Run for your life as the clanging bells
toll the nightmare stalking the earth.

MOURNING

Tell me how to stop the grief
that grips at my heart
and so blinds my eyes
with tears I cannot see
the brightness of the day
nor the promise of tomorrow.

Can you assure me with Spring
my tears will thaw my anguish
and I can lift myself up
from the darkness of sorrow
to feel again the sun healing
my pain-ridden heart?

LAMENTATION

Flesh of my flesh, blood of my blood,
you suckled on the nutrients of my body,
growing from a tiny seed into a burgeoning
root that pushed from my womb into the world,
red like a ripened beet, opening your lungs
to inhale the air of life, screaming your objection.

I held you in my arms, gently as a precious gem
that might disintegrate into dust if I pressed
you too closely to my breast. But there you were,
the fruit that grew from the soil of my body,
always to be my other self, never to be severed
from that umbilical cord that wraps around my heart.

As you grew, I taught you to walk in this world
unafraid, I taught you the courage of manhood,
I held you close and said *love, never hate,*
for that will destroy you. I tried to implant in you
my heart, my soul, but I wanted you to be better than I.
I prayed that God would care for you when I could not.

And then, my son, you surged into manhood with love
and patriotism in your heart. You sprouted upward
like a strong limbed tree believing in brotherhood
and the veracity of your country, unable to understand
the evil in this wanton world. I had taught you love,
the world mocked you for your weakness.

When the country you loved called you to sacrifice
your life to fight the evil that had exploded, unhesitantly
you agreed. How could you do otherwise when I
had taught you love of country. A part of me died
when you left my embrace, but perhaps I have been dying
a bit each day since you left the security of my womb.

Heart of my heart, flesh of my flesh, they took
you away like a lamb to slaughter. They put that gun
in your hand and said "kill". If I had taught you the evil
of this world, would you still be alive? Oh, my son,
the umbilical cord wrapped around my heart
is squeezing the blood from my body!

THE IMMORTAL TREE

(In memory of my father)

The tree has been felled. The old
beloved tree, so bent by the wrathful
winds of life, has been severed
by Thanatos' remorseless axe.

It fell not with a thunderous crash,
nor with dust spewing from its roots,
but quietly to the cold, hard ground,
its branches never again to whisper
endearing songs in the evening breeze.

O, but see the saplings sprouting
from its ancient roots! They suckled
of its sap and now grow strong and tall,
surging into immortality.

IN MEMORY

You are not dead, dear friend,
you are the evening star that haunts
the setting sun, the moon within
whose depths I see your shining face.

You are the seed from which
my dreams first sprung to life—
my teacher, idol, inspiration,
my hope of greater things.

You are not dead, dear friend,
you are the breeze that dries
my tear-stained face, the swallow's song
that echoes softly in my saddened heart.

THE FINAL FLIGHT

(Triolet)

The eagle spreads its wings but cannot soar
Into this night to make its final flight.
Its wings are motionless forevermore.

The eagle spreads its wings but cannot soar;
Its piercing eyes no longer can ignore
The shadows that annihilate its sight.

The eagle spreads its wings but cannot soar
Into this night to make its final flight.

THE IRREVOCABLE

No more to write of peace and love and brotherhood.
No more to sanction man's pervasion of the earth
for God has lost the fight to repossess man's soul
and Satan rules the earth with flaming sword held high,
an exorcist of all that once was just and good.

And through all this God waits outside the rim of night
defenseless in His love to save His anguished world,
but when the flames lick at the stars, His tears stream down
like ice-encrusted rain upon the steaming chars,
making them hiss like countless fiery-tongued snakes.

Thus, man, the instigator of his own calamity,
sent up one last beseeching scream to God.
But all too late his supplicating cry for absolution,
the devil trampled on the earth with cloven feet
and God was deafened by the roar of burning souls.

Alexandra Moss Zannis

I WALKED IN YOUR SHADOW

I lived on the edge of your limelight,
Half in its geometrical cone;
I trod in the wake of your footsteps
Unaware of the prints of my own.

You surged through your life like a comet;
I trailed like your vapor tail;
You plowed like a full-masted schooner
While I was the jigger sail.

But now all the lights are extinguished,
The stage is abandoned and dark;
The flame of your life has been severed
Like a match that's devoid of its spark.

I walked in the shell of your shadow
And forgot that its shade would not last,
And now when I tread in the sunlight
My form has no shadow to cast.

SHADES OF PAIN

In the prime of my youth, I stood at the foothills
gazing upward into those towering mountains
that stretched into obscurity, knowing
that I must climb them all. But I was young
and you were beside me, motivating me onward
into the hidden promises of my future.
>   Ah, sweet pain, propelling pain.
>   You fired my body with the fuel of love.

In the mid years of my life with you at my side,
I rested at the pinnacle gazing down
upon the perilous path that bore us
to this heady height. The route we'd traveled
filled my soul with awe that together
we had succeeded in our lofty goal.
>   Ah, pensive pain, propelling pain,
>   you fused my body with the fuel of attainment.

At the diminishing days of my life, I fell
from those lofty heights, my body careening
down the precipice into the devastating
depths of death. You were gone. My strength
poured from my pores like a fissured dam.
>   Ah, agonizing pain, propelling pain,
>   you flooded my body with the tears of extinction.

TEAR DOWN THE SHRINE!

The mourning is over.
Tear down the shrine.
Face reality and know the past
for what it was. Ignore the rage.
Remember the laughter,
remember the tears,
but tear down the shrine!

There's only the urn,
his ashes are gone.
Long have they sunk
to the Aegean's abyss
and snatched by Poseidon's hands.
The mourning is over
so tear down the shrine!

Blow out the candle.
Let the wax cool
and shape it with finality
in the palm of your hand.
Snuff out the fire
for the flame is no more.
Tear down the shrine!

THE BRILLIANCE OF THE STARS

(Τα Αστρα Εινε Λαμβερα)*

Τα Αστρα Εινε Λαμβερα. Remember, my love?
Remember that time in our youth when we walked
the ship's deck on that ink-black night?
We leaned against the railing and stared up into
the heaven brilliant with its myriad blinking stars.

They belonged to us that night—all the stars
and the blue-white moon. They were ours as we stood
body to body, hand clasped by hand and surveyed
the beauty of our future in those "λαμβερα" stars.
But now you are gone and the sky is black!

Τα Αστρα Εινε Λαμβερα! No, my darling, the stars
are dead! The moon is a cold, smirking face mocking
the memory of our love. Where is your hand
to press against my beast? Where is your body to feel
your strength giving me the fortitude to live?

O, dull, lifeless stars, glow with brilliance for me once more.
O, cold, smirking moon, let me soar once more through the heaven!

- (tah astrah eenay lahmberah)

BONES

The flesh, after many years
in its tightly-sealed tomb,
has decomposed and now the bones
must be removed from the sarcophagus,
scrapped, cleaned, washed and left to dry
in the sun-flecked shadows beneath
the cypress trees edging the cemetery.

A gentle balmy breeze softly stirs
their branches, filling the air
with a soporific sound simulating
a hushed lullaby, so as not to waken
the dead in their crib-like crypts.
But today the bones are removed
and purified for their final resting place.

All that is left is our bones. Where once
beauty reigned, where once we trod
the earth in human form, where once
we looked with vanity upon our bodies,
in the final reflection we are only
the edifice of that calcium deposit that now
lies drying beneath the cypress trees.

HOMOPHOBIA

On October 10, 1998, Matthew Shepard
was brutally murdered because he was gay.

They left together from the bar, pretending
they, as he, were gay conspirators,
drove far into the countryside and dragged
his slight-built form (*just five foot, two and weighing*
but a bit above one hundred pounds)

from out the car across a moon-drenched field
where there they lashed him to a buck-rail fence
and without mercy pistol whipped and spat
upon his face and torso, loathing what
he was: a harmless homosexual.

His battered, bloodied body was discovered
eighteen hours later bound upon
that fence and thought to be a scarecrow
dangling there: a symbol of what hate will do
when bigotry corrupts the human soul.

Alexandra Moss Zannis

LAZARUS RESURRECTED

Arising from the grave
where I had mentally buried you,
you stirred, pushing up through
the illusionary soil, shedding
the shroud I had wrapped
around you, and looked
into my eyes reproachfully
as if saying "why did you
try to bury me when I'm
still alive?"

Oh, I did not want to bury you!
I wanted you to live,
but seeing you so comatose
I did not wish you to suffer.
I only wanted what
I would demand for myself
if my life no longer
had value and I lay listless
unable to respond
to life.

When you opened your eyes,
eyes that once again blinked
with life, you lifted yourself
up from death, stood,
wobbly at first,
and took that first step
into the realm of the living.
Ah! Leo Maxikos, my beloved cat,
like Lazarus, you have been
resurrected.

THE LAST FAREWELL

(to my beloved cat)

I held you in my arms as the fluids of death
flowed into your body. I kissed your
beloved face and watched your life ebb
from your pain-filled body, knowing
no longer would you suffer.
I gave you death as your freedom.

If only my decease would come so easily.
If only I could say "Please end my life,
I wish no more to be a part of suffering.
I've lived a life with no regrets. I've loved
and suffered pain and happiness."
Why would I ask for more?

Sweet Leo, as Horatio said to Hamlet.
"May Angels Guide Thee To Thy Rest"
and give you peace and solitude as you lay
in the grave where I placed you, forever
to remain a poignant image in my collage
of unforgettable memories of love.

WITHOUT HOPE

All the days of her nights
Were as eclipsed as the darkened suns;
Each breathe that she drew
Was bile in her languorous lungs.

All the nights of her days
Had no beacon to light her way;
She stumbled through life
With feet that were formed from clay.

Every night of her life
Dragged endlessly into the dawn.
There existed no seed
From which any hope could spawn.

At the end of her life
When darkness expunged her sight,
She went to her grave
And into that tenebrous night

MY FATHER WORE TROJANS

When I was a child I remember one day
snooping through my parents' bureau drawers.
I had no business there but curiosity was one
of my weaknesses. While rummaging through
one drawer I discovered a little red tin box
with the head of a man wearing a strange helmet.

I held it in my hand and worked laboriously
to pry open the lid. Inside were these small
wide-necked balloons. Wow! Were they
to be a gift to us girls or just hidden away
to be blown up for the 4th of July? I tried
to blow one up but had not the breath to fill it.

My curiosity sated, I placed it back in the box,
closed the lid, shut the drawer, and forgot
the incident . . . that is, until one day, while trying
to grope for something that had fallen
under their bed, I had to crawl on my back
to reach whatever it was that had rolled there.

And then I saw them: those little wide-necked
balloons! There they were stuffed between
the mattress and the springs. Dozens of them,
all dried up, brittle to the touch and looking
very depleted. Why would my parents blow
them up and stuff them under the mattress?

As I grew older and learned the purpose
of those little balloons I couldn't blow up,
one memory kept flooding my mind:
the memory of their bed so often crashing
to the floor. Those little balloons stuffed between
the mattress and the bed springs were the cause.

A PREFERENCE OF BEDDING

It seems in Indiana in the Spring
Flower bedding is the only thing
That everybody has the urge to do
To give their lawns a prize-awarding view.

But I, I'm just a misplaced city gal
Who has no interest in the rationale
Of flower bedding when the Spring breaks through.
In that regard my mind has not one clue.

I say that flower bedding's not for me.
I'd rather spend my time more happily
In bedding where true bedding ought to be:
Between the sheets with a manly bonhomie . . .

NOBODY CAME TO MY FUNERAL

Here I am, Dead! So where is everyone?
In my will I arranged a fantastic funeral
with Vivaldi and Bach to be played. No open casket;
only a simple coffin to hold my ashes.
No body to be buried in the insect-infested earth!
Why honor the worms with such a feast?

So here I am inside my urn, reposing quietly
atop this ludicrous satin-lined coffin,
waiting for mourners (or even my enemies)
to walk down the aisle, glance at my photo with love
and respect, even hate or sneers (no spittle please!),
then return to their pews in respectful silence.

My God, how many funerals I've attended!
Now where are all those "hypocrites" I paid respect to?
I said my farewells when each of them kicked the bucket!
I'd like to emphatically say to them now "Drop Dead!"
but since that's what they are, it's what they deserve
for not being here to respectively say goodbye!

A great bunch of friends and relatives all of you!
Here I am, my last day on earth
and you haven't the decency to say farewell!
Well, what can I do? Is it my fault
I lived to the age a hundred and two?

THE LAST BEQUEST

Here he lies at last in peace,
Hands folded on his chest,
And just before his sad decease
He left his last bequest:

To you, my spouse of many years,
Who drove me to this plight,
I rid myself of one last fear
By selling your gravesite.

The thought I'd have to lie beside
You til eternity
Did make me happily decide
That that would never be.

So now you'll have to find your own
Sweet cemetery crypt
And when you lie there all alone
Just keep your big mouth zipped!

MASOCHISTIC LOVE

Oh, the pain of being stretched upon the rack,
To feel the snap of my sacroiliac,
With arms and feet restrained and leather strapped—
I yearn to be so utterly entrapped.

Bend my body, make my bones to crack:
This torture is my aphrodisiac;
No greater pleasure could there ever be
From each salacious jab you give to me.

Bear down upon my back your iron fist,
For such intolerable pain I can't resist;
Contort my body, give me *jois d'esprit*,
I'm in the utter throes of ecstasy!

I spend my days in unrelenting stew
Awaiting for our future rendezvous.
This truly is a most significant factor:
For I'm enamored with my chiropractor!

I DRINK TO DEATH

I raise my gin-filled glass to death
And toast whatever waits for me.
I drink to that last labored breath
That leaves my body gratefully.

I'll lift the beaker to my lips
Loudly proclaiming death be damned!
l swallow all in grateful sips,
Down to that last delightful dram.

I'll leave morticians in chagrin
By facing death without a qualm,
For with my body filled with gin
There'll be no need to be embalmed!

THE ITCH TO PLANT?

I've scratched all night and I've scratched all day
But that itch to plant won't go away.
I eye those clods in that hardened soil
And my hands go numb when I think of toil.

So I lean my hoe on the garden fence
And wait for the weeds' benevolence.
The itch to plant? Well, I must admit
I've rubbed on salve to make it quit!

THE PLEASURES OF SCOTCH

You can take my Cartier jewels,
You can take my Rolex watch;
But please, dear God, don't take away
My ever-lovin' Scotch

* * *

Pour me three ounces of J&B
And I'll say what you want to hear;
But pour me a pint of that sociable Scotch
And I'll whisper it in your ear.

CURIOSITY

Of all the boys I've ever known
(And there really were quite few),
I liked the best the little one
Who was a darling Jew.

I've often wondered how I came
Upon this grave decision.
But then I guess it all boiled down
To viewing his circumcision.

THE JOYS OF WINTER

What joy to see the falling snow that sheets
the frozen ground. It covers all the earth
and hides the ice with such discretion
we never know it's there until we slip
and fall upon our heavily-padded rumps!

And then the thrill of driving on ice
when tires skid and the car whirls about,
not knowing where it will stop,
if upside down, or slam front end into
a car that's coming down the other lane.

Could riding on the roller coaster make
adrenaline race faster through your veins?
And the joy of living through a storm
of ice and snow when all electric wiring
lays dead upon the ground and there's no heat

for days to warm your cold and huddled body.
If the joy of winter is what you want,
then I suggest you move your overheated
carcass to Glacier Bay, Alaska, and frolic
there upon the glaciers before they melt!

IN A 'CLINTONIZED' MANNER

Now what do you do with a guy like Bill
Who was king of the road on Capital Hill?
He strayed from his duties
And got caught in the 'nudies'
'Cause his mind over matter was nil.

Poor Bill has been crucified by the press
And Starr made sure there was nothing suppressed.
But B.C. was noted
To have cryptically quoted:
"It was only a 'Clintonized' jest."

NO TEARS FOR MONICA

Why weep for Monica, she knew very well
She put Bill at risk with her kiss and tell.
You don't lift your skirt
In a casual flirt
And expect a man's genes not to swell.

O, Monica, Monica, you've passed the test
Of luring a president onto your chest.
The Oval Office is not
Where to start a sex plot;
It's there that the Chiefs keep 'abreast'!

THE JOY OF A YOUTHFUL BLADDER

As I patiently sit on the porcelain seat
And wait for my bladder to ooze,
My deep concentration is rudely assailed
By the clatter of high-heeled shoes.

A door is yanked open with a powerful jerk
And the seat is slammed down on the stool.
Within but a second I hear with a gush
The stream splashing into the pool.

While I am still waiting to finish my task
I hear from the neighboring stall
The flushing of water, the opening of door
And those heels clicking down the hall.

Alas, here I sit deploring the plight
Of this truly significant matter.
And then I remember when I was young
And the joy of a youthful bladder.

MY OLD HOUSE

My house was constructed in '38
And then it fell in a dreadful state.
Now that old house is younger than I
But my old body is still quite spry.

The house was reroofed and the plumbing repaired,
While *my* head's well thatched and my pipes well cared.
Do you think if I'd doused it with Vitamin E
It might have stayed sturdy and as strong as me?

Now I am told that the wiring's gone bad
And I'd have to replace it or lose my pad!
So I mortgaged my soul from stem to stern—
But I should have let the damn house burn!

TO A CLEAVAGE

Oh, softly swelling breasts that dare protrude
So tempting from a décolleté neckline,
What metaphors can thus the mind allude
To paraphrase this image so divine.
Is this the cleavage that was formed at birth
Or did some clever surgery occur?
Did artificial means increase their girth
Or is it genes to which we must refer?
Yet we without this luring subdivide
Wish no ill-will upon those so endowed,
And if we seem to be a bit green-eyed,
It's thinking we are lost within the crowd.
    To all those ladies with their cleavage grand,
    Do not deride my slurs, but understand.

A JOYFUL ENDING

Perhaps it was a thoughtless lack of judgment
In choosing food that now within me vexes.
My innards feel a definite begrudgement,
For something gurgles in my solar plexus.
What I consumed I have no recollection;
Was it some cabbage or a garnishee?
But I do fear that soon it will take action:
An indiscretion it will surely be!
What shall I do, I'm at the bursting point;
I'm tightening all the muscles in my rump.
It's building up into a counterpoint!
Ye Gads, I can't control that blaring thump!
    Although I have performed this bold disgrace,
    Complete contentment's written on my face.

TRUE LOVE

In olden days some lovers did insist
Their maidens wear the belt of chastity.
They feared their true love's failure to resist
Some other knight who spoke more wittily.
If true love is the moral of this tale,
Why did he doubt his lady's chastity?
His mission was to find the holy grail
And trust completely her veracity.
Poor maids who thus so senselessly endured
This iron gadget locked around their waist;
What mortal sin could ever be incurred
When in such ridicule they were encased?

 Dear maids, no need to agitate herewith
 Just find a good dependable locksmith!

LOVE'S COMPETITION

In days of yore a maiden would find love
In a muscle-bound and hairy-skinned athlete.
She modestly let fall her dainty glove
And hoped young knight would pluck it from the street.
Such chivalry one never questioned then;
Hers was a ruse of femininity.
For in those days it's said that men were men—
One never probed their masculinity.
And now it seems that gender's dubious,
His countenance may mask a certain trend;
He may appear as strong Prometheus
But with his eyes he's seeking other men.
　　In search for love, a maid must now compete
　　With muscle-bound, and hairy-skinned athletes.

THE SHRINKING SKIRT

Once ladies wore their skirts down to their feet
As modesty was then the golden rule.
A lady always had to be discrete
Or if not so, she'd bear the ridicule.
Then fashion slowly changed with passing years
And inch by inch the hemlines reached the knees.
If this apparent shrinkage perseveres
What vogue can curiosity appease?
Alas, there was no stopping of this trend
And ladies soon exposed their fleshy thighs.
The moral is they really should not bend
When wearing such a tantalizing guise.
    But I confess, how can one not but stare
    When bending, they expose their derrière?

THE DESIGNER MAN

O, seek you well the latest fashion trends,
You men of Gucci, Prada and Dior.
Their luring ads attempt to make amends
For what's amiss in bodily décor.
Those jeans that cling so tightly to your thighs
And emphasize convexity of groin,
How can a maid withdraw her staring eyes
From such a tempting image of your loin?
But if of bandy legs you are inclined,
(As if from round a horse those legs were formed)
Beware of what the stylists have designed—
In tight-fit trousers you will look deformed.
    So, men, before you wear the latest fad,
    Make sure your male physique is ironclad!

THE AGE OF CLONING

It seems that cloning now is quite the rage
When of yourself you wish posterity.
If in this plan you covet to engage,
'Tis best to travel with timidity.
Please ponder on this nuclear transfer:
What if a donor egg would be replaced
By accident with that of some wild cur—
Would you then be eternally dog-faced?
To risk this catastrophic accident,
I think would wiser be to hesitate.
If of this wistful dream you can't relent,
Could wolfish howls forever be your fate?
  O, vain-filled man, do not this thought pursue;
  Who wants to scoop up after two of you?

THE MARRIAGE VOWS

In current times, the marriage vows have changed;
No more we hear 'til death do we thus part.'
A quick divorce is easily arranged
If murder is the canker in your heart.
When once we heard 'I claim you man and wife'
We now attune our ears to other vows.
The words of 'he and he' are running rife,
And 'she and she' no longer raise eyebrows.
If this is now our new society,
How are we to distinguish who's to rule?
It once was known with notoriety
That men were masters without ridicule.

    When females pair our thoughts become askance—
    We wonder which of them will wear the pants.

THE HOLY WORD

To doubt or to believe, that is the question
That skeptics often ponder greatly on.
That subject can engender indigestion
For fear not knowing what their views will spawn.
If bended knee in prayer you do discredit
And shun the words the Bible does proclaim,
You may upon your deathbed much regret it,
For who can know the ending of the game?
To all you disbelievers hearken true,
The unknown firmly grips us in suspense.
I think it best if I but do advise you
To feign at least a holy countenance.
    'Tis wiser if upon the Word you dwell;
    Why risk the chance of going straight to hell?

THE PLAYBOY CENTERFOLD

So beautiful a body to behold;
Would Venus ever dare to strike such pose?
A carnal beauty is this centerfold
Of flesh more lustful than a wanton rose.
Her luring curves beseech one to explore
The attributes of her anatomy.
Can one resist from being predator
In seeking out what's there for all to see?
O, hearts that pound a syncopated beat,
O, fervid moisture flowing down one's pate,
No other vice is nearly half as sweet
As viewing that which can intoxicate.
 So, dear young boys, clutch close that magazine
 And with locked door devour that lustful scene.

THE SERPENT

The serpent tempted Eve to eat the fruit
From off the tree God fervently forbad.
"There is" he hissed "no flavor more acute
Than this arousing morsel to be had."
Eve tasted of the fruit that flamed her groin
And Adam too partook of that delight.
And when the two did lustfully conjoin,
God knew their sin and forced them from His sight.
Tho' Eden is but just mythology,
That serpent does assuredly exist.
He slithers forth in sly cryptology
Between the thighs of maids who can't resist.
    Dear maidens, to this fact you must concede:
    To shameful sin that serpent will you lead!

FOSSILS

When dinotherium creatures disappeared
Their bones lay in the earth a million years
And formed that gaseous substance so endeared
By gas-consuming engines and their gears.
When once the wheel was introduced to man,
The mode of travel turned from feet to horse
And then from horse to engines there began
The race that had no halting in its course.
One thinks of all the mammoths that have died
To feed our guzzling gas tanks to the brim.
If in this undue digging we abide,
The future of the engine does seem grim.
    With SUVs and the soaring price of gas,
    I think it's wise to view the horse's ass!